W9-BXZ-431

MORNING RUN

MORNING RUN

POEMS BY

Jonathan Galassi

PARIS REVIEW EDITIONS

BRITISH AMERICAN PUBLISHING, LTD.

Many of these poems were published, in somewhat different form, in the following periodicals:
The Antioch Review, The Atlantic Monthly, Canto, Harvard Magazine, The Nation, The New Republic, The Paris Review, Pequod, Ploughshares, Poetry, Poetry Nation, PN Review, Shenandoah, Some Other Magazine, Southwest Review, Three Rivers Poetry Journal, The Threepenny Review; *and in the anthology,* Ten American Poets, *ed. James Atlas (Carcanet Press, 1973).*

Library of Congress Cataloging-in-Publication Data
Galassi, Jonathan.
Morning run.
I. Title.
PS3557.A387M6 1988 811'.54 88–16821
ISBN 0–945167–05–9

CONTENTS

Your Words

for Susan

There are words
in everyone.
Often they go unspoken
and die with their maker.
Few of us know our own,
though some spend their lives on imitations.
But you found yours
in the dream when the great man told you,
"The fragile part of your language
is mutual."

Those were your words, not his.
You let them into the world,
you threw them down, a challenge to answer.
We don't know if they're true, but they're poetry,
a responsibility.
And nothing we say, awake
or asleep, can take them away.

ZEPHYR

The silver light that shines on the floor
through the branches of the silver birch
is watery because the sky
is full of water. Spring has arrived
in its usual difficult careless way,
backing and filling, blowing hot and cold,
mucking things up.
You could be its zephyr with your cheeks
ruddy and bursting,
aloft and leaning into the change,
the new breeze pushing the curls at your forehead back,
brave like a snapping pennant
or a kite defining the currents over
the soggy fields, or charting the boundaries
in your sweatsuit on the horizon,
hard to make out except for your lope,
your canter which can be read
for hundreds of yards like the words
they trail over beaches in summer:
READ THIS, DRINK THIS, DO THIS . . .

BE THIS, you seem to be saying, BE
A PART OF THIS, as the naked trees
sway in their willing way and the young sun
still fails to break through the strength of the clouds
hovering over the parti-colored crowd,
and gusts of not-unfriendly wind transport you
everywhere, though nowhere we have been.

ELAINE IN EDGE CITY

Up above the city it has rained
and little droplets shimmer everywhere
as if there were angels in the air
waving their mica wings and starting fires.
I'm standing at the porch rail holding tight.
Out here the wind is cold and strong tonight.

The night is wet and cold and the cliffs fall
at least a thousand feet below my feet.
Down in the dark some loud suburban queen
has spread her gaudy phosphorescent rocks
on satin for as far as I can see.
And out beyond them somewhere is the sea.

They say the smog has covered up the bay.
If our ship comes in we'll never know,
but would it make a difference anyway?
Everyone keeps an eye on the horizon.
What's there to wait for, what could she possibly bring?
Last time I counted we had everything.

I take the freeway and go wandering
down in the valley, on the hunt for buys.
I find better bargains every day,
but everywhere it's the same merchandise,
the same tie-ups in the parking lot,
the same paying for what I've got.

Things disappear and other things appear.
Cobras in pairs predict a coming tremor.
Suddenly, they're curled up in the drawers,

safe in the mountains where they can't be swallowed.
Locked in the car, I read and wait for rain.
When the weather lifts they're always gone.

Summers the firehorns keep going off
north of us in the hills. I watch the smoke
shift in layers on the heat and head
to sea. Below the haze whole miles burn black.
At night the hummocks glow like bedded coals.
I go out on the rocks for midnight strolls.

I listen to the ocean when the moon's
down and the house stops creaking in the wind,
and stillness moves in like another breeze
and faintly in the distance something breathes
like a baby. I'm inside a shell,
cradled in the rhythm of the whole

world turning, humming like the bass
on a radio playing down the hall.
I roll over and look down on the lights
steady below me, blinking as I blink.
I think I hear you breathing by the bay
under my hand, just steps away. I say,

Come in.

IF ANGER WERE POWER

I want to hold on to the hand of the man
who is stronger than I am, feed on his energy.
I can't look him in the eye. When I do I see
blue crystal, dangerous sand.

I want to shake off the weight of the man
who is weaker than I am, who's about to drown
and holds me back,
who shivers when I take in breath
and shrivels when I stare him down.

If anger were power, not the loss of it—
an engine revving on an empty tank,
a ghost of power—the weak would put on armor
and the strong in being strong
would have a double.

If anger were power,
we'd either all be dead or locked together
in peace we can't imagine, bound to love
the little lives we ruin when we move.

TO A CLASSIC POET

You had the world confirm your fantasy
that what you felt was common and uncommon,
that something in you might go into words.
You're not that boy today, who felt
all-powerful and unforgiving,
but what you tossed off then survives to haunt you,
petrified, unforgettable.

Your leap of faith might have been ridiculous
if you hadn't landed feet first.
From hindsight we called it prodigious
and the fool became a saint.
Schoolchildren recite you, not even your worst,
but you don't want to hear them,
it's not you anymore.
Now you pace off a remoter landscape,
far less hospitable, but the view is endless.

You bask in the freedom of silence.
To you it's punishment.
You'd rather be in the agora,
sweating with the rest.
But something took you up and carried you off.
The words of a moment—
your moment became ours—
fought their way into a life
that doesn't care about you
and has to be made to see,
has to have its nose
rubbed in reality.

And afterwards doesn't matter.
What matters is the now that doesn't change.
Given the choice, you might have kept your distance.

BEAUTIFUL LOSER

19th-century family picture

The menace of success, the likelihood
of failure—things I don't dare get near.
A man sits at a desk for thirty years,
detail upon detail, resolving
into years . . . *"Only success*
makes confidence, and only confidence"
is handsome, tall, well-spoken, dressed to kill.

Your strength was in your look, illusory.
But even in your photograph I see
the eyebrows sag, the mouth about to give,
a blur of helpless hands, which proves
you can be talented and loved
and lose
and disappear.

That was your program: promise and demise,
ambition foundered on a tide of claims.
Young you were golden, favored cousin,
eldest son of elder brother.
And you carried it with grace:
cupidity, angelic in your face,
made them adore you. Mother has the note
her grandmother's Aunt Ethel wrote
saying in Bath they thought you were "a card."
But that was years before you strapped
the family future on your back
and stole away. One morning you were gone.
In one night you became the man
no one heard a word from in a lifetime.

It's said your disappointment took you south.
Maybe you met another woman there.
Something in me imagines you
a large success under an alias
in a muddy, raw post-bellum town,
a small-time patriarch without a past,
hoary, with a row of grandchildren. . . .
But does that count, becoming someone else
somewhere else?
Here you're what your picture says you were:
a strong, mustachioed, beautiful young man
who ran away.
No one "keeps" your memory,
tells children what you felt or said
or, beyond leaving, what you did.
The faded paper proves you lived
but nothing of you lasts:
no chiselled face, no uniform,
nothing changed or written, nothing to confirm
the threat you were, the gifts your fear survived.

OUR SKY

Its livid, living, through-the-windshield blue
shatters whatever separates us from it.
The sky is here: substantial, clear
—though pocked with light at night
or hidden from us by rain
till the plane lifts out of the clouds and the ceiling emerges
just as unsullied, just as always there
as if it had been imagined.

Driving west the great tent of the sky
has to be seen: an ocean swallows the flatness,
blistering, billowing, an egg erupts
in a blue bowl so constant in its flawless
shapelessness it says eternity,
perfection, wholeness, like the water
it shares its color with, so wide and right
there's no competition.

But it doesn't exist: it's ours.
We take it to bed with us, paint it,
it papers the walls of our rooms:
pure blue or pure blue tinctured with six-point stars,
half-moon above the altar or half-barrel
studded with heroic constellations
or pale—almost a green—over the concourse
or striped with kites or birds

—it's ours: where manna falls, the spirit's home,
the place we're going to or coming from,
the square or rounded boxtop that
we think we feel by morning light

and later as it leaves us, and at night
when one red dot beating from left to right
repeats, "It's there,"
hiding the unbelieved, uncolored rest of space

behind a scattered screen of mackerel clouds
or white exhaust or other kinds of glory—
baby blue true mirror blue or inky
an ethereal or a drowning blue:
our roof, our depthless unreflecting pool,
clouded or still depending on our mood,
depending on the weather in the world.

MONTALE'S GRAVE

Now that the ticket to eternity
has your name on it, we are here to pay
the awkward tribute post-modernity
allows to those who think they think your way

but hear you only faintly, filtered through
a gauze of echoes, sounding in a voice
that could be counterfeit; and yet the noise
seems to expand our notion of the true.

An ivory forehead, landscape drunk on light,
mother-of-pearl that flashes in the night:
intimations of the miracle
when the null steps forward as the all—

these were signals, sparks that spattered from
the anvil of illusions where you learned
the music of a generation burned
by an old myth: the end that will not come.

There is no other myth. This sun-drenched yard
proves it, freighted with the waiting dead,
where votive plastic hyacinths relay
the promise of one more technicolor day

—the promise that is vouchsafed to you, scribe,
and your dictator, while your names get blurred
with all the others, like your hardest word
dissolving in the language of the tribe.

TO ZACHARY

You can see the mountains from your window
—I mean the hills, the old mountains.
Gray and blurring in the August heat,
ageless and unchanging to us, they've changed.

And the cooling breeze that always blows off the hill
and over the lake where you like to fish with your father
is probably bitterly cold in winter,
but we're not here in winter.
In our city beds we can dream the endless
acres of ice and the flawless drifts,
not the trouble they mean or bring.

The world unfortunately isn't
this farm that isn't a farm,
this field where nothing happens
but the wind and the rain.
And you know it, though you're still a child:
you want to be watched when you swim into deep water;
the flies that circle your father's sweating head
anger or scare you.

I'm still a child myself
but somehow I'm carrying you
up the hill. You're twice as heavy as you were last year.
The bank is strewn with little strawberries.
You know how they taste, both tart and sweet,
you know how they feel,
and that we sometimes bruise the fruit as we climb,
and that its blood as we do is staining my heel.

THE LAKE

If we could see the lake someday without
the heaviness the clouds are always casting
in pewter ridges, would there be a doubt
our temporary life is everlasting?
Our temporary life, the one with days
and weather and a future made of same,
of springtimes, noontimes, new beginnings, ends,
till we don't see the water for itself,
the image for the thing that isn't there:
not the towel on the plastic chair,
not the paddle propped on the canoe,
or the trout at sunset rising to
the bait of a mosquito,
but everything that these and we suggest:
ideas, forms, abstractions, qualities
that hover somewhere over them like haze.

There's a cold morning shadow from the trees
that you swim out of, heading for the sun.
Light on the crest of the water plays and plays
when you break the seal of the surface with your hand
to shatter an appearance, recreate
a chaos, as your arm sinks in the lake
like teeth in meat, the way the element
partly resists and partially gives in
and you move forward on the difference,
leaving a wake of diamonds, froth and noise
that lasts an instant, which is comforting
or chastening, depending on your mood.
But who could want to leave a name in water?
What's brilliant is your interplay with sun,

the crystal palaces, jeux d'eaux,
animated sculptures and light shows
you make up through a little mutual
exertion, with no thought of shape or sense.
Lie back and kick, the others do the rest,
the golden rainbows fall across your chest,
and their distinction's their impermanence.

Back on the dock you're back in the world of shadow:
dew on the chairs and darkness in the trees
where life, that made so much
commotion in the trash last night, is lurking.
The critters think the world belongs to them
and maybe it does:
you can shine a light in the lake at night
and see the snakes arrow out from the dock,
trying to disappear
so our world won't intersect with theirs.
Nature is crowded: every inch
crawls with crossed imperatives.
Listen and you'll hear the little death cries
salt what you thought was silence.
No wonder everything resembles something
else, no wonder waves across the water
read like a message broadcast from the core
till every story
is an allegory,
and unforgiving afternoons
when everything the self is not
gathers in a livid knot
over water black with clouds that loom
(clouds that are saying something, only what?)
face it: there are no things but in ideas,
and the whole world is this empty room.

But here in the blond morning
who remembers yesterday's storm?
Fred is out taking the boat for a run, a few
canoes and colored sails are making background.
Everything's intent on being warm,
everything we see bespeaks enjoyment.
The water's gentle changeability
is constant, a release from entropy,
a way of blocking all the messages
or else a gathering of messages
into a tutti: endless rise-and-fall
and come-and-go, all one, all one, all one. . . .
Yet the pale imagination
colors at the thought of something brighter
and more abundant than this risen world:
the blueberries just dropping on the water,
so many birds the silence terrifies,
and the drinkable lake, so pure your hand is bigger
and broader in it, purer
with pure blood running in untrammeled veins.

PRESENTISM

The world has got so crowded, is there room
for anything that used to be the past?
The present has invaded every tomb
and cave and temple ruin in this vast
dig of ours with its electric broom,
swept away the ancient dust and plast-
ered over its cheap paper and made a home,
white-walled, well-lit, foursquare, slipshod and fast.
The present knows it's living through a boom,
that it can't let a moment go to waste
if its cool neon's to erase the gloom
from those unvacuumed halls where shadows cast
by old highboys and mirrors used to loom,
enlarging the bent shape of things that last.

THE LOOK OF THINGS

for Katha Pollitt

1.

It isn't worth our while to fret about
our excellence or impotence in art.
I would have liked to be wilder, bolder,
someone who had tampered with tradition,
more personal or more impersonal.
I could have used a better body, too,
and a more classic profile;
but then I would have been a different person
and written other poems, if I'd written.
For our real poems are already in us
and all we can do is dig.
We can work for years and never find them
or miss them when they stare us in the face.
At the worst (which is our common fate)
we turn up rubble:
bits of dirty mirror, shadowy glass
that tells us nothing,
market value absolutely nil.
We can keep on digging, as we will.
But we were trained enough to recognize
the jar was flawed, cracked in the firing,
and when we started to fool with it it shattered
into infinite slivers no one can put together.
And each of them gives off the same small light.

2.

But you say art's extrapolation from
the jagged markings on those bits of clay;
we can invent them into undulant
lines on perfect jars mysterious
women once brought to aromatic wells.
I thought the nineteenth century taught
the past we fabricate is parodied,
Alma-Tadema or, at best, David.
Look at the eye of this Egyptian boy
some unknown Roman caught in paint:
something unimagined, history,
not seamless or idealized—a face.
What strikes us in the image is the damage.
Here was a wound no hex could heal.
Flies danced around it on warm days,
no amount of incense hid the stench.
And as for what it saw—
sewers, beggars, sheepshit in the muck,
tainted water, starving children, sores,
women dead in childbirth, other women
hauling water for the fire at home.
This was the world your jars were modelled in;
is there no hint of it in their design?

Who wouldn't have his youth back if he could,
not to live it better but relive it,
those exquisite mistakes, just one more time.
Your poems say you would, although you claim
that art is office archeology.

Yet somehow I read something else
in your beads and bits of glass:
imperfection, rage, remorse,
innate late twentieth-century loss.
You know your only archive is your life,
your past; its embers glimmer in your lines,
which may, if we are lucky and survive,
become a piece of this time's evidence
when our quaint habits, primitive machines,
outlandish clothes and more outlandish notions
furnish the future's sense of the pristine.

Katha, the wine that you and I
keep on professing we want to drink
won't tolerate pure vessels; it corrodes.
Its bite is modern and it goes by names
unheard of in the purlieus of the shardsmen.
It's not the palmy gardens of the brain,
their bright-tiled, nonexistent walls,
your women and their plangent chant
that you say underlie the look of things;
our province is the plain:
its now and endlessness, heat, occasional rain,
and, from a slow rise, the long view
over scrub pine and factories
toward something faintly made out on clear days:
maybe mountains, maybe haze.

CONSCIENCE

after Natalia Ginzburg

Then we start to grow away from our old friends.
Their pretensions and refinements have become annoying.
Their mania for distinction is bourgeois.
Now we want to be poor. We make poor friends,
visit them with pride in their unheated houses.
We take pride in our beat-up raincoat.
We're still waiting for the right person
but she will have to love our old raincoat,
our beat-up shoes and cheap cigarettes and bare red hands.

Evenings we walk alone in our raincoat
past the houses at the edge of town.
We have discovered the periphery,
the signs of snack bars along the river.
We stand entranced in front of store-windows
hung with workshirts, overalls and long underwear.
We're enthralled with old cards and hairpins.

Everything old and poor and dusty calls to us.
We stalk the city, hunting the authentic.
It's pouring but we stand bareheaded,
soaking in our leaking raincoat.
We'd rather die than carry an umbrella.
We have no umbrella,
no hat, no gloves, no money for the streetcar.
All we have in our pockets is a dirty handkerchief,
crushed cigarettes and kitchen matches.

THE ESCALATOR

I saw you on my way from shoes to sweaters
coming down the escalator in the gray suit
we had bought together in Venice.
It had been years but its cut was still stylish,
and your hair had the dark color of that summer.
You didn't see me,
though I waved, and even called out your name
—maybe not as loudly as I might have,
but people were beginning to notice,
and I'm not sure I really wanted you to see me.

At the next floor I turned and walked back to the escalator
to try to find you.
As I rode those slow steps, expectant, anxious,
helpless in the crowd,
I saw you again, but closer,
so close in fact I think I could have touched you:
you were standing on the near side of your step.
But you stared ahead, self-absorbed,
your eyes set clear and still.
I saw you were younger,
younger than in our first days
when the Greek light hurt your tender skin.
You were younger, fresher as you passed me
than even my most remorseful memories could make you.

I turned at the next floor
sensing that if I followed
I might see you again, travelling in the opposite direction,
still younger, more radiant, more fixed.
I saw ahead an endless stretch of afternoons

wasted while I pursued
your waning, perfecting image on that escalator forever,
your forehead forever purer, your gaze more firmly set
while creases and pounds slowly gathered around me.
And I knew there was no chance of meeting,
no chance of proving you real,
of going to where we could take off our things and lay down
some of our imperishable differences.
I knew I had no chance to learn to love
something of yours that wasn't flesh or voice
or gesture, or even simple presence
—something more changeless or unchangeable,
more essential than your open eye.

AGAINST EARRINGS

Don't tonight, don't wear
perfume or put up your hair
or do any of those things
that we do for disguise.
As if earrings could change
you into someone strange.
Don't you know I'd know your face,
its ivory veiled by your hair,
in the grave? I'd reconstruct
your brow, the deep lines backing away from your lips,
your cheeks, your modelled chin.
The brain's that way:
once the pattern's etched the song just plays
over and over, deeper into the plastic,
till it's worn out or broken.

What we love is what we recognize.
Those four arm-in-arm in the street
are so similar: tanned, expensive,
bonded closer than brothers.
And how do we look to others
in our paleness, our glasses and ties?
Where we see *interest, intelligence,*
the world ignores us, passes by.
Everyone makes out his own:
the snake eyes the snake,
the swan swims next to the swan.
I'm like you now, I'll grow more yours with the years,
taking the imprint of your features on
till in the mirror we're almost the same,
two cracked vessels with the one design

brimming over, pouring
into the other.

But tonight the mirror says we're still young,
our friends are at home, the shades are down in the room.
Take off your necklace, earrings, rings,
don't take off only almost everything.
We're here in our common perishable raiment
less beautiful than we've been but together,
flawed but appreciable,
and better than we'll ever be again.
Come as you are, let's practice the routine:
contour into contour, life into life,
over and over in each other's hands
turning and returning, a Moebius
strip joined who can say where?—
one side forever
trying to be the other.

SAVING MINUTES

You were in bed.
You heard your mother working in the kitchen.
It was still light, the birds were bickering,
the waterfall behind the house was falling.
Its rushing lulled you,
you loved the moment you lay in,
and you counted the time
from this instant

to this,
and put it away
to be lived on another night,
your wedding night or some other night
that needed all the luck,
all the saved-up minutes you could bring it.

Later you filled bottles in the stream
and dated them and stored them in a cupboard.
Months after, you retrieved them
to stare at what time had done.
You were eight, but already you knew
it was working on you,
each minute you passed through was gone.
You didn't want to give up your old clothes.
You'd watch your mother wrap
your dresses in a box for another girl
and know that where their stripes and buttons went
what you'd lived in them followed.

But those minutes in bed,
minutes of utter safety,
you heard the water falling
and didn't want it to fall.
You wanted to keep it,
you saved yourself that minute.
I don't know if you still have it
or if you've had to spend it
on you or on me.
But I know you still save minutes
I used to think went unwatched
into the bank in time
that allows no withdrawals.
You hold onto the slippers and letters,
things that are leaving, things we've left,
evidence we're judged unfairly by.
You have the picture, you and Pam in blue
fishing in the stream below the pool,
staring back at the camera half-abashed.
Your jacket is still in the closet.
You never wear it,
you don't even remember when you did,
but it's here to testify
the picture doesn't lie
—though the color's different,
your hair is shorter now,
and the water in the pool
is long gone downstream.

GIRL ON A BIKE

Block Island, R.I.

Shirt around waist, your rumpled ducks
and faded sneakers pumping up and down,
you meet the challenges the day creates:
the hills that rise up when you leave the town

and keep on coming while you thread the fields
decked out in goldenrod and up the lane
to see the swans that dot the hundred ponds,
and me behind you under threat of rain.

You make it happen: suddenly the sun
steps from behind the arras of a cloud.
You're at the crest and all there is is sea—
sea and wind that make the silence loud.

And coming down the counterbreeze you make
plays havoc (gently) with your streaking hair.
The weather smells of heather, salt and effort,
art is artless and the world is fair.

AFTER INGRES

The high white bodice with its silver silk
ribbons strains against your rising breasts.
Your hair, pulled back, is dark against
the crisp and pale-as-eggshell air,
and your full lips are faintly pursed,
with expectation, is it, or disdain?
Behind you, the hometown you haven't left,
down to the littlest window
and crack in the church plaster,
falls under scrutiny.

Mature, you're settled in a high-necked gown,
pale skin stark on ochre
brocade of your pillow, while the book
lies face-down in your lap.
Only the finger pressing your cheek
indicates your fabled restlessness.

Three-quarters, middle-aged,
ensconced in silk and mirrors, powerful,
reserved, urbane, the brocade on you now,
you're fuller, bright eyes glazed
with the glare of knowledge, with satiety,
your pearl-gray flounces livid with a sheen
that might be photographic—

I want my art to be this linear,
rational takes of you in your changing phases.
Not approximate splashes
whose chiaroscuro suggests
the musculature of an arm

or an obvious feeling.
Not empty unknowable faces.

Realities:

each eyebrow beetling, arched or pencil-thin,
each cheek laid with actual down
or pocked with the diseases of these years;
each finger jewelled precisely as it was.
Everything soft or kind or hard or cruel,
everything taken for granted, as we take it:
your mouth, its pout or grimness or relief,
its fact, picked off like fruit and laid down flat
in painting that professes impudence
and smacks of frankness even when it lies,
even when it flatters,
even when it falters,
in color with the order and the luster
of ordinary light.

IN THE POOL

for J.A. and A.F.

That sweltering night of your wedding in Vermont
we all went down to the pool behind the barn
with no light but the stars.
The two Bobs and Richard wanted to go swimming
so they stripped and dove
into the chilly water, hooting and jeering.
That made the rest of us brave
and one by one we set aside our drinks,
took off our ties, suits, socks and shoes,
fancy dresses, watches, underwear
—everything—
and jumped or waded into the water.

All that liquor and the unnatural heat
made it even colder.
Some of us actually swam
or threatened to splash the few recalcitrants.
But mostly we just stood there in the dark
talking or calling each other across the pool,
or sat on the rough rim feeling our sweat mix
with the water streaming down from our hair.

All those ambitious people in one pool!
Old enough at last to be old friends,
that night we forgot everything but each other,
naked together in black water
under the spangled, solemn Vermont sky.
Later we got used to the light.
Our whitish, thickening, still-limber bodies
glowed faintly in the shallow pool,
younger or otherworldly, ghostly,

like Anna's blade-thin dress
making its way up the hill.

An image made for memory.
We cherished it without knowing,
staying and staying
until it started to get cool at last.
And then we came out and put on our clothes
and stumbled across the dark lawn to the cars.

OUR WIVES

One rainy night that year we saw our wives
talking together in a barroom mirror,
and as our glasses drained I saw our lives

being lived, and saw that time deceives:
for we had thought of living as the Future,
but here these lovely women were, our wives,

and we were happy. And yet who believes
that what he's living now *is* his adventure,
that the beer we're drinking is our lives?

Think of all the pain that memory leaves,
things we got through we're glad we don't see clearer.
Think of our existence without wives,

our years in England—none of it survives.
It's over, fallen leaves, forgotten weather.
There was a time we thought we'd make our lives

into History. But history thrives
without us: what it leaves us is the future,
a barroom mirror lit up with our wives—
our wives who suddenly became our lives.

AFTER WORK

you sit on the couch in your green
sweater and tell me
what you feel.

I stand at the edge of your picture,
a cool place,
leafy, tangled,
your words around me.

I want to enter,
dissolve in their stream,
move into that hidden pool,
deeper, clearer
than anything here.

What holds me back?

Not your sun-struck colors,
so close they could be mine,
or the long alley of elms
that crosses the middle distance
or the surprising line
of statues, their pedestals
carved with strange names.

Sister, it's me. Keep talking.
The same old story's
better every time.
Go on. I'll watch the pebbles
come alive in the water,
shift in their bed.

Flow. Pour.
I'll lie by the basin
bare in the breeze
and let you spread
the honey on the bread.

GUILTY

I'm daydreaming of our future walks
in the garden down below the house
that it takes all those flights of stairs to reach
and the long morning mists off the water that mean
the blossoms come at you, cadmium red and white
out of the haze.

This is to be in the years when our children have flown
and we're free for months to contemplate
clipped hedgerows, topiary and
the temple on the island that no one visits.
It's hard to see why order
can make us think we understand the world,
because in spite of straight streets
and the curtain that always comes down
chaos is forever seeping in.
Nature itself is better at this
because it offers us so few
illusions about ourselves.

The question is: can the human be beautiful?
The garden says it can,
and every act of yours (almost)
refines the spirit, turns
the mind inside this aging flesh around.
From very early I was sure I was evil
and everything I'd accomplish
could never undo the bad.
But watching you be
means there can be hope for me,
and the garden lessens the dread a little, too,

if we sit on a bench
by a pot of lavender watching
the vistas get made.

I wish you could take our world
or even our little back yard
and make it an image of yourself
a fury of color and doubt
with no self-consciousness
and not one trace of artifice.
We could escape there into our own nature
—if nature is still nature,
still not ours, not poisoned by our presence,
if the brook breaks over the rocks
as purely as something of yours
stands forth and the air is clear
as your eye or your candid walk.

I remember the scent
of your dew when I first knew you
so pure, so gently salty,
a whiff of another being,
and no deeper perfume could equal
its mild sublimity.
It was what told me you were part of nature.
I belong on the other side of the line,
guilty,
an agent of destruction.

Yet I feel I have more respect
for sublimity than you.
Maybe you take it for granted,
being natural.
To me it's divine,
yet you're casual with divinity,

with the cosmos. Potnia Gaia,
you yourself are a garden
where I have planted.
Make the world outside the same while you can.
Cultivate our little patch.

SOUTHAMPTON

The light comes back to gild the trees
later than this across the pond,
bringing another green to these
blue precincts, burnished in the grand
tradition, like the wider leas
of sky that imitate the land,
far more expansive than the sea's.
Some intimations never end.

But later you came back and found
that even if the light will stay
there's no disturbance in the sound,
no late boat out to make the bay,
only a few birds circling round
looking for how to end the day,
uncertain when to come to ground.
Some intimations die away.

And what remains is immanence,
the silver-gold traced on the blue,
the wind that makes them come and go,
and the horizon line that bends
to gather as the shadows grow
the sails, the fields, the birds, the friends,
all but the eye that stays with you
when the last intimation ends.

A PARIS SUITE

1.

Sometimes the clouds run off and the stone lights up
cascades of contrast on the old facades
you think will last forever it's so deep
and old: old European light
someone called mother-of-pearl.
You cannot cross the rich grass of the past
you have to come from behind
on your narrow path
in your heavy coat
while your heavy breath tries to rise.
So leave it for the primrose and impatiens.
If summer comes
the all-pervasive issue of the moment
—clouds or sky, water or clear air—
dissolves in the general heat and windlessness
and the bricks of the Place lie flat in the sun
and the old question re-occurs
(it does even tonight from under the snow
that lasts as long as it takes to cross it):
something about yourself and the powerful
lord on his high unimpeachable horse.

2.

From the top of the mountain today you can suddenly see
the towers surrounding the city.
The walls don't exist any more
but we could be medieval citizens
in our winter cloaks and boots
the kind of scribe
who sits at home and copies in weak light
or wanders on the cobblestone and straw.

The day wastes itself.
Only your red umbrella
enlivens the aquamarine
bedspread, till the Alsaciennes next door
start laughing and the courtyard lights are lit.
Parisian night.
Then you come in and we go out
to watch the French stars dodging the rooftops.

3.

The strongbow you draw back when you enter the garden
is aimed at the heart of the palace guarded by soldiers
who are younger and braver than you.
The vista almost stretches out of sight
but you walk it, you bring it to its end
halfway between the rows of upraised fists
and the male and female gods
symmetrically disposed at the points of the compass.

Man is everywhere in his divine
aspect: his cold white flesh
is stark against the winter green
as you scatter the lovingly raked sand in the twelve directions,
proud to be something disordered and out of place
foreign, like the tree that leafs out of season
the one fountain that somewhere is playing.

4.

The sad gaiety of the hand organ
if you hear it
changes the afternoon
into something with a depth
a wound you can get into if you want to
or a screen with a life behind it
like the smoky blue of the sky that reminds you of elsewhere
where you felt less circumspect, without division.
Paris is another word for home
but not in your language.
For you it is the sample in solution
the skin dyed radioactive.
You hold it up against those semi-
abstract pictures the sky keeps painting
kaleidoscopic forms that imitate
the crowds adrift around
the post-electric building.
But the rain falls in your oysters, thins your wine
so you walk the locked-up streets, not really cold
till something develops, you go inside
and one of you is finally big enough
to cancel the other.

5.

And then the gentle moment comes
or seems to come.
The air is the same temperature as you
or seems to be,
a little wind just barely stirs the leaves
that have appeared.
At night you walk along a wall
and smell a garden on the other side.

It will be cold again, the sun will be
impossible
(even today he seems to threaten to)
and the rain will return with its storms
to shatter the roofs long after you're gone.
But something in the moment promises
a kind of truce
a way of life that isn't always
terror and compromise.
Like everything, it always breaks its promise
and comes back to remake it not even abashed
not even with its tail between its legs.

Yet tonight the royal alleys blaze around us
under a half-open sky.
The constellations blink
in the light fields over the clouds—
a sign, a dare,
a rearrangement in the air.
Another piece of the world

that says it fits and does because it says so
offers its exaltation here and now.
We're brave for once tonight,
stare back and take it in,
watching the glare of winter disappear.

VINTAGERS

The blistering hillside choked with thirsty vines
that swallow up the valley by the mile—
who could spend a life and labor here
shirtless, bending and plucking single-file
where sediment and sweat corrode the air
and the huge fetid merciless sun shines?
Not you or I; but there are men whose lives
are measured sowing in this acid soil,
who till and trim and root and wait for rain
that the all-too-perishable fruit not spoil.
They know what *toil* and *bread* and *daily* mean:
their hands have harvested the grape that gives
a blood not unlike water, and supplied
the native thirst that's never satisfied.

STILL LIFE

Somewhere you're always twenty-four
and lie on sand
so hot I have to stand still
before I can move.
It's early but your tan is Arab-dark,
your hair incongruous blond.

A body rich in possibilities
like every body: you had longish hands
and wide eyes, blurred by something
you had to reach to feel.
Part liquor, part intelligence,
it might have been real.

At the little lake you knew
we were silent
while the blood-red sun
rang down on the scenic view:
white barns and a tree or two
in the fly-blown water.

We could have cracked
its mirror with a rock,
a branch that might have lifted
something muddy to the surface.
Instead we kept on staring
and the sun set, several times.

WONALANCET

At the lookout, hacked away
a shaft of clarity
cuts the thick heat

somewhere out there
three yellow patches on the nubbly green
meet at two corners, trapezoidal, neat
undesigned:

a new place, unshrouded by the mountain.

And then you make it out: the house
(that spot in the corner of the nearest field)
the spire, cars on the Sandwich road

and distance
stretches down like a wire
from this sudden window in the mountain

—reducing what we reeled about at night in
(far from the houselights
reckless, as if we could roam
forever on that floor)

until the dewy, black, unmown
emptiness becomes
a bright thing I can cover with my hand

undoing what we climbed for:
summit

space
vibrating unnamed away from Whiteface

forest, water, haze
all our taint erased
in the moment no truck moves in New Hampshire

and nothing touching us
nothing near but air
nothing that we have to know we know.

LATENESS

Lateness is all that shimmers in the leaves,
that trembles in the bending grass,
that glistens on the berries on the vine.
Even before the final glut of summer
there is an inkling of the coming wine.
That gentleness of sunlight on your cheek
is a last kiss, the silence in the trees
is one last breath held back before September
sharpens its shears for pruning and a chill
unpolishes the surface of the lake.

Lateness is all: the aura of Before
is telling you to take stock in the fall
because the season's fruit is not for you.
It is still basking, rounding on its stem,
still tied to life, but you are looking on
into the conflagration that will come.
Last days are fire and water while the grape
is gathered and its sweetness is expressed,
and every afternoon's a little less
expansive, till the gold days are gone.

Are you ready to be harvested?
When all the weeds of summer have been mown
and raked away, will you be staying on
like the high apples, lasting in the trees
for the long vistas of the final days
and the immense sharp stars? Will you be here
still breathing in the temple of the air
and seeing through the bonfire of the fall,

where being and having been are everything
and lasting is all, you know that lateness is all.

KING CAESAR'S WINDOWS

The shipyards of Ezra "King Caesar" Weston at Duxbury, Massachusetts. were the largest in America at the turn of the nineteenth century.

The Gurnet beacon shudders in the distance
off Powder Point, caught in the soughing wind.
King Caesar's windows keep their watch forever
over the empty water of the harbor
where nothing moves except the brown sea reeds
bending the wind's way to the open east.

The blank black panes stare out on the flat east
as if a ship lay anchored in the distance
hidden behind a thicket of sea reeds,
waiting for a favorable wind
to carry her into the shallow harbor
to berth among the pleasure boats forever.

King Caesar's crafty workmen were forever
building boats. The best fleet in the east,
some say the world, sailed out of his trim harbor
bent on some sweating seacoast in the distance
where a dark cargo waited in the wind
that shook their shackled bodies like thin reeds.

King Caesar stayed at home behind the reeds
watching his masts go up, the gold forever
growing in his countinghouse. The wind
smelled of his rumrunners from the east
carrying contraband, built to outdistance
challengers. At home they hugged the harbor.

King Caesar knew the currents of the harbor.
He learned the weather from the waving reeds.
From his front parlor he surveyed the distance
for his white sails, richer than Aegeus, forever
watching for sons returning from the east,
his pilgrim jaw set firm against the wind.

The thin windows rattle in the wind
and look out blindly on the glassy harbor,
expecting ships long lost to the wild east
to tie up suddenly among the reeds
and serve their master as they had forever.
Implacable they stare across the distance.

Dories knock in the distance. An east wind
fills the dark harbor. The brown sea reeds bend
before the windows as they have bent forever.

ELMS

to a teacher

Your "yet-to-be-dismantled" elms are few,
and by the time you read this may be gone.
In my own childhood we had one or two
over the lawn, before the hurricane—
tall wineglass trees too noble to survive
a time like ours, too stately or sublime;
something in us wouldn't let them live.
Or was it simply that they'd served their time?
"The size of our abidance" wasn't theirs,
the way it can't be yours. That is a trait
of nature, as it is a trait of ours
to see in something passing something great:
our backwardlookingness that makes a tree
the genius of the place it used to be.

SAN FRANCESCO

Here where the figs are falling from the trees
here in midsummer where immortal flowers
pepper fields that yesterday were green
and ten varieties of vine
threaten to engulf the old garden
and what you thought was silence gives
into patterns of humming: flies, mosquitoes, bees—
here where the steam is rising off the hills
to hide the mountains in a mystic haze
(not to mention all the scales of bells)
you start to see that years are days.

I won't say the litany the trees
give off with their names, varieties of sun
and sunset that the broken wall gives back
or the fluidities the landscape makes
into motion. I can't imitate
the narrow line of cypress going up
the hill in the dark, or how the glade below
seems to offer its fruit like a bowl,
still and whole,
pale and full,
or the dark tower above or the saint in the window.
I know it's all imprinted on you too
and you can bring it back with just the name:
what the memory of a place can save,
how it reflects another part of us
without a warning, when we least expect it.

MORNING RUN

Villa Doria Pamphili, Rome

Often you start the day here, when the sun
is softest, having only just begun
climbing, and the lowest foliage steams,
clearing itself of nightsweat and the dreams
of the old city waking into heat,
crowdedness, poverty, terror, human dirt.
You dodge the lines of traffic where you can
and jog up to a neoclassic span
of russet stucco crowned with limestone lords,
arms, and abbreviated Latin words
memorializing Innocent,
who "pamphilized" Rome, then past his monument
and under shade along an aqueduct
through which St. Peter's cupola—the top
alone—gleams like a gazebo or a teahouse
adrift in farmland, eloquent and senseless,
and veer left at a second, smaller gate
through undergrowth and past the headless late-
Imperial boy in an embarrassed pose
to come out on a scraggly field where rose,
bluebell and poppy manage to be seen
amid tall grass, no longer really green.
The orangery that brackets the Casino
is eerie, sun-dazed, bleached and empty now,
its maze of formal gardens gone to seed,
the terra-cotta tubs profuse with weed,
the walkways overrun, the statues down,
like the old town of tombs the house was built on
—and the facade, all filleting and frieze,
peeling and opulent in the thin haze.
Belrespiro, where the favored came

for respite from the heat and stench of Rome
to breathe free in a nature they could mold,
symmetrical, humane, rich and controlled,
all disappearing now in ripe confusion,
waste and disparity, the baroque tension
of topiary, marble, sky and trees
lost to corruption, disarray and ease.
Eight o'clock and there is just a breeze
stirring the tallest ilex, papal bees
are working in the flowers and the birds
are filling up the silence with their words.
The emptiness reverberates as air,
light, heat, scent, color, timelessness: desire.
You gather energy and take the stairs—
leftover heads and bodies everywhere—
three at a time to reach the fields the boys
will pepper later with their games and noise
and shirts and hair, as lover paired with lover
will lie down in the grove beyond and hover
between decorum and abandon, spread-
eagled together on the needle bed,
while down the hill the pensioners complain
over their *bocce* in the shady lane.
In a low wall you find another gate.
The fields beyond are wild, unmown, and yet
water is running in the knee-high straw,
fountains are playing somewhere, someone saw
an order here, too . . . and you make it out:
the lake below, its curve that swings about
halfway through the vista like a scythe
and finds its echo in the twining, lithe
limbs of Bernini's several mingled writhing
nymphs, who mock your fervor to embrace
the weather and the moment and the place.
You are alone here, yet you seem

verging on some encounter, some deep dream
surfacing in which the body tries
to become nature and the world complies—
a fusing with the air, a loss of self
into an energy that could be life,
a surging forward to become the wind,
hunger no experience can end
half satisfied in being body, sweat,
speed, color, an equivalence of heat,
while the repeating rhythm of your feet
synchs with your breathing till it is your heartbeat
and the land you're running on is ocean,
rising and falling, fluent with your motion
until you can believe you are the day,
you are the sun that brings life and decay,
that warms and soothes and in a moment turns
merciless and withers, burns.
You keep on running, closed inside your breath's
spondaic trance of oneness, power and health,
follow the ragged trees, as overgrown
as your own eagerness for the unknown
which threatens to spill forth at every turn
until you rise once more to a new plain,
another level, a new rush of pain,
and sprint down an aisle of poplars to a barn,
which was the goal.

And now you must return.
You round the mottled walls, the moment shifts,
the sunlight broadens and the last cloud lifts
over Monteverde, where the day
is gathering its errands. The caffes
are crowding and the gates are going up
over the shopfronts. Time to call a stop
to your exuberance, time to be tame and calm.

The morning's work is waiting in your room.
You leave the park to other runners now.
Trapped in their heavy clothes or else extreme
in their expertise, their search for form,
they seem to need to work against the heat,
but you for once luxuriate in sweat
as you lope halfway down the hill to home
and bath and coffee, and one look at Rome
from the window, laid out like a brain,
its crenelations steaming: your demesne,
or so it looks this morning, from this height—
who knows the colors it will wear tonight?
You gaze again, then shut away its din
and face the table, ready to begin.